AIRSHOW USA

PHILIP HANDLEMAN

Dedicated to my mother and father

Published in 1988 by Osprey Publishing Limited
27A Floral Street, London WC2E 9DP
Member company of the George Philip Group

© Philip Handleman

British Library Cataloguing in Publication Data

Handleman, Philip
   Airshow USA.—(Osprey colour series)
   1. United States. Aircraft
   I. Title
   629.133-0973

ISBN 0-85045-884-6

Editor Dennis Baldry
Designed by Paul Butters
Printed in Hong Kong

Front cover The USAF's Thunderbirds Air Demonstration Squadron are enthusiastic operators of the F-16 Fighting Falcon multi-role fighter. Mounted on the F-16 since 1982, the team has previously utilized the F-84 Thunderstreak, F-100 Super Sabre, F-105 Thunderchief, F-4 Phantom and T-38 Talon

Title pages One of the many Texans, in this case a Marine Corps SNJ, which graced the parking area during the 16th annual Gathering of Warbirds at the Madera Municipal Airport in central California

Back cover A Pitts S.1 of the *Holiday Inn* aerobatic team is pushed back to the parking area after displaying at the Gathering of Warbirds airshow

Right A Ryan monoplane, similar to the beloved PT-22 Recruit, taxies to takeoff position during the World War 2 light trainer fly-bys at Madera. Note the lone cockpit, speed ring and wheel fairings

The 1987 American airshow season, extending from March in Florida to November in California, was an unforgettable experience for me. In all, during the course of the season, I attended nearly thirty shows and fly-ins. The real world of business pressures and personal obligations had a way of intruding on those long weekends, pulling me away from the charmed life of casual dress, hangar talk and new-found flying friends.

My enthusiasm for airshows and indeed of aviation itself stems both from a young boy's natural fascination with flying machines and from hearing my mother's stories about the historic Cleveland Air Races, which she attended in the 1930s while growing up within walking distance of the then annual event. After years of patronizing airshows, even flying in some, I decided the time had come to compile a permanent record of an American airshow season.

Of course, this book is not that desired record for the countless sights, sounds and emotions from the galaxy of airshows of a full season can hardly be captured in the pages of a single volume. Be that as it may, this book hopefully conveys at least a flavour of the American airshow circuit as it exists today. Hopefully, too, it will touch that same nerve of adventure in the reader, young and old, that prompted me to take up flying.

During the Edwards Air Force Base open house celebrating the 40th anniversary of supersonic flight, some humorous sorts with the Air Force Flight Test Center demonstrated their wit by offering a few accessories as a display of the as yet unseen Stealth Fighter. Its pilot, except for his flight boots, is equally transparent

Contents

Fly-in fun

Left Wayne 'Walt' Pierce rattles a lazy Florida sky in his souped up Stearman, *Ol' Smokey*. Accompanied in wild formation by a partner in an identically decked out Stearman, Walt's airshow act was a popular attraction at the 13th annual Experimental Aircraft Association Sun 'n Fun Fly-In

Above Deceptively quiet during a balmy afternoon, the Stearmans of the Red Baron formation aerobatic team await their turn to roar impressively over the anticipatory Sun 'n Fun crowds at Lakeland, Florida. Altogether there are four look-alike Stearmans that comprise the Red Baron team. It is unusual, but excitingly so, to see a formation aerobatic team of such number employing the bulky Stearman

9

Top left Contact! This is vintage flying the way it really was, as Dean Tilton (barely visible) shouts the magic word from the rear cockpit of his beautifully restored Travel Air 2000. Requiring more than one throw, the lineman's handpropping finally prevails and the antique, after a few coughs, fires to life

Left The Travel Air is rich in the lore of aviation. Handed-down stories and faded lithographs have helped immortalize this frail looking airplane as a vibrant part of the fabled Golden Age of Flight. When this diminutive shape, with its distinctive elephant-ear ailerons, puttered down the taxiway under an inviting Florida sky, the aviation enthusiasts assembled at Sun 'n Fun gazed at it admiringly

Above The design genius Walter Beech produced the classic Staggerwing. Ahead of its time, the Stag featured an aerodynamic teardrop shape, an enclosed cabin, retractable landing gear and 'I'-shaped wing struts. The wings have an unusual negative stagger, which means the lower wing's leading edge extends forward of the upper wing's leading edge. It was an uncommonly fast airplane for the late 1930s, even able to outrun many military types of the period. This immaculately restored Stag occupies a special place amidst the rows of show airplanes at Sun 'n Fun

Overleaf Another sparkling Beech Staggerwing at Sun 'n Fun. Note the shine produced by the polished spinner

Left Joining the company of Staggerwings in the tie-down circle for special restorations at Sun 'n Fun is this stunning Stinson Reliant. Often called the gullwing Stinson, for obvious reasons, this type was a sturdy workhorse in an earlier era. This gullwing Stinson has a bumped cowl, rarely seen these days. A special touch is the duplication of the fuselage trim stripe on the wheel fairings

Above The rudder lettering identifies this brightly coloured aircraft as an SNJ-6. Today's airshow circuit is attracting many more newly restored trainers. This one, seen under a sky dotted intermittently with puffy cumulus clouds, had plenty of Texans as company at Lakeland during Sun 'n Fun

Overleaf, left Eddie Andreini thrilled everyone at the 23rd annual West Coast Antique Fly-In and Air Show at Watsonville, California with an amazing routine in his highly modified Stearman. Horsepower was more than doubled with the installation of a Pratt & Whitney 450 horsepower engine. The cockpit was fully enclosed by a specially manufactured bubble canopy. The already durable aircraft was further stressed for high G loads. Andreini, who is a regular performer at the Watsonville Show, actually put his super Stearman through a wrenching outside loop. Here he dives for speed after some wild gyrations that apparently have confused even the smoke trails

Overleaf, right If you blinked, that was a climbing roll! Contorted smoke trails in the sky are Eddie Andreini's trademark

Top left Airshow performers make their job look easy, but only because of the seemingly infinite number of hours of preparation and tender care provided their equipment. Eddie's magnificent machine gets a thorough going over in between his performances

Left During the course of the American airshow season one is liable to come across a few examples of this beautiful rare biplane, referred to affectionately by old-timers as the Bird plane. Its distinguishing feature is the enormous camber and span of the upper wing in relation to its meager sized lower wing

Above A Watsonville tradition is that Jim Nissen kicks off the airshow portion of the annual Fly-In by ascending ever so slowly in his lightly powered

Curtiss JN-4 Jenny with a skydiver aboard. Built in 1918, the Jenny is among the oldest airplanes flying today. An example of its authenticity and frailty is the tail's touchpoint which is a wooden skid. The World War 1 biplane therefore always operates from sod fields. When displayed on pavement, as shown here, the precious and delicate antique is pushed and pulled, not taxied, to its parking spot with the help of a two-wheel cart (partially visible behind and below the empennage) that elevates the tail so that the skid does not scrape along the unforgiving asphalt. With care like this it is no wonder that the pieces of timber in this Jenny are in outstanding condition and are probably collectors' items themselves

Overleaf While geared to the ragwing owners, a small number of the comparatively heavy metal airplanes, like this Navy SNJ, show up at Watsonville

Top left Many fledgling military cadets were initiated into the flying fraternity at the controls of a Ryan PT-22 Recruit. This one enlivens the Watsonville flight line with its bright custom paint scheme

Left Although twin-engined, this Cessna 'Bobcat' Bomber is a fabric covered airplane. The California sky behind it shows just a trace of clouds

Above This is an extremely rare 1946 Johnson Rocket, restored over an eight year period by Orval Fairbairn. This post-war design boasted high performance at a reasonable price—a combination the Watsonville group and others in general aviation would happily settle for today

Right This view from the tail shows off the sleek lines of a kit built airplane, the Glasair III. It is the newest in a well-regarded line of very fast kit built aircraft. This modern general aviation design, incorporating some of the latest design concepts and aeronautical technology is at once both a departure from and a reminder of the myriad antiques stretched out along the Watsonville flight line

Left Another post-war design was the Navion, this one sporting a snappy two-tone colour scheme that matches well the clear sky over Watsonville. Although not fast, it is sturdy. Originally targeted by North American Aviation for returning military flyers, the Navion built a loyal following but did not catch on as hoped and so after continuing ownership changes from one manufacturer to another production eventually ceased

An array of biplanes from across the United States colourfully decorates the Bartlesville, Oklahoma landscape as the National Biplane Association convened its first annual Fly-In

Top left Bartlesville is the home of the Phillips oil dynasty. Fittingly, a Phillips fuel truck laden with avgas quenches the thirst of a Fly-In Stearman

Left A possible future Stearman pilot contemplates his miniature flying contraption, in an apparent effort to master the axes of flight

Above The Boeing Stearman Model 75, in its multitudinous variations and corresponding designations, served as the US military's leading primary trainer during World War 2. So many thousands were built for the training effort and then after the war such a large percentage were operated as crop dusters and sprayers that today the Stearman is the most common biplane in the United States. Not surprisingly, Stearmans dominated the National Biplane Fly-In. Oblivious to the world only a few hundred feet below, this Stearman cruises lazily on a hot June afternoon. Perfect open cockpit flying weather!

Above The Bartlesville gathering saw an amazing assemblage of brilliant restorations, like this fire engine-red Stearman

Top right Often mistaken for a Stearman, this is an N3N, conceived and constructed by the US Navy as a primary trainer. The N3N, along with the Stearman, was known in the Navy as the Yellow Peril. Among the features that distinguish the N3N from the Stearman are the aileron connector struts aft of the 'N' struts between the wings

Right Only occasionally seen these days is the Meyers OTW. Not that many were built, but those that appear on the airshow circuit are almost always in good shape—perhaps reflecting their non-use as crop dusters and sprayers. Unlike their biplane brethren, the Meyers OTW fuselage was made of metal. The powerful afternoon sun glistens off of the polished skin of this example

Above Of course, a national biplane fly-in would not be complete without a complement of Beech Staggerwings. This one sports a protruding spinner

Top right Two Navy Stearmans in formation pass low over the airport at Bartlesville during the annual national Antique Airplane Association Fly-In. The lush green hills in the background nicely silhouette the Stearmans. For many years the AAA held its annual Fly-In at its headquarters—Antique Airfield near Blakesburg, Iowa. But because of the short grass runways there, some would-be participants did not come. The decision was made to rectify this inadequacy by changing the venue of the annual Fly-In to an airport able to accommodate all antique airplanes. The ultimate choice was Bartlesville with

its 6200 foot long runway. The airport had been used earlier in the year by the National Biplane Association for its first national Fly-In. Also, the Bartlesville Chamber of Commerce displayed special interest in attracting additional visitors to the local area during the petroleum industry's doldrums

Right Amid rows of beautifully restored aircraft at the AAA Fly-In rests a Ryan PT-22 Recruit. This airplane has been restored with some authenticity for its metal fuselage has been left bare while its wings and control surfaces have been painted high visibility yellow. Its rudder has been painted in alternating red and while stripes with a single blue perpendicular stripe

Top left A Travel Air beauty at the AAA Fly-In. The big wheels, overhanging ailerons, speed ring and spinner are the stuff of which flying dreams are made!

Left Quiet and unassuming Bob Greenhoe's one-of-a-kind Pasped Skylark. Invariably, wherever he lands his special airplane with its bulbous wheel fairings and other distinctive features a crowd of curious onlookers huddles around it peppering Bob with questions. This picture was snapped in a rare moment when the Pasped Skylark stood alone

Above Tail feathers! The world's largest post-war gatherings of Stearmans take place each September at the Galesburg Municipal Airport in west central Illinois. This year nearly one hundred of the venerable open cockpit trainers, including the author's, were in attendance

This immaculate Stearman, the proud mount of Harry Thomas, is a standout among the many sparkling restorations at the Galesburg Stearman Fly-In. Fitted with a 300 Lycoming engine, this beauty sports a full cowl, polished spinner, wheel fairings and a headrest. The blue trim nicely accents the shiny yellow of this past award winner. As in earlier days, an open cockpit biplane like this might be seen over adjoining cornfields, with the wind whistling through the flying wires and a silk scarf flapping in the slipstream!

Oshkosh, by gosh!

Left No other flying event evokes as tremendous an outpouring of enthusiasm for aviation as the Experimental Aircraft Association's annual Fly-In at Wittman Airfield in Oshkosh, Wisconsin. The week long Oshkosh extravaganza draws upwards of 800,000 spectators. Behind the ever-expanding EAA Museum is a quiet refuge—an airport within an airport. Pioneer Airport is an EAA creation, devised to resemble a 1920's airstrip. It is home to a panoply of gentle old ragwings many of which are maintained in flying condition. On summer weekends, the flyable antiques can be seen taking to the sky via Pioneer Airport's tiny grass runway

Overleaf, left Robert A 'Bob' Hoover—combat veteran, former test pilot, peripatetic airshow performer—streaks across an obliging Oshkosh sky. As part of his routine in the Shrike Commander, he performs a slow roll after intentionally shutting down an engine

Overleaf, right Sponsored by a pizza company, the all-black Red (?) Baron Stearman team strut their aerobatic stuff

42

Above Smoke on! A thrilling moment at Oshkosh—four wingwalkers at once! From left to right: Gene and Cheryl Rae Littlefield, Bob and Ruth Blankenship, Bill Barber and Eddie Green, Bob and Pat Wagner

Overleaf A quiet interlude for one of the several wingwalking Stearmans at Oshkosh

43

Duck! Here comes Leo! Aerobatic champion Leo Loudenslager can do just about anything in his super agile Bud Light. He is seen performing an inverted ribbon cut and, at a more comfortable altitude over Wittman Airfield, a knife edge pass

47

It is an understatement to say that Eagles team members like to fly close. During opposing solos and crossovers it appears that the airplanes touch each other

Above It is a tight squeeze into the cockpit of the BD-5, the world's smallest jet aircraft. The two pint-sized jets of the *Coors* team can be seen with the Oshkosh control tower looming in the background

Top right Lifting straight up on takeoff, this AV-8B Harrier dazzles the crowd at Oshkosh. Just think what Leo Loudenslager, Bob Hoover or Charlie Hillard could do with one of these!

Right A reminder of EAA's roots, these homebuilts occupy centre stage at the Oshkosh Fly-In

Overleaf The breathtaking North American P-64, a frequent airshow mount of EAA founder Paul Poberezny. In typical EAA fashion, this rare warbird has been restored and is maintained so meticulously you could feel comfortable eating off its wings

Top left In keeping with Oshkosh's reputation for drawing unusual designs, a Transavia Airtruk arrived to grace the flight line. Curious spectators swarmed around the odd looking utility aircraft. Reportedly, it hauls oil field workers and supplies to remote drilling sites in Australia

Left This quintessential World War 2 fighter—the North American P-51 Mustang—is part of the enormous Oshkosh warbird contingent

Above Peeling off over Oshkosh! On top is Donald Davidson's award winning Mustang *Double Trouble*

Reno:
air race
and
airshow

Hot and heavy—throttles full forward! At the 24th annual Reno Air Races, Lefty Gardner is at the controls of his distinctively all-white P-38. Skip Holm is piloting Joe Kasparoff's P-51. Reno is synonymous with speed. Each year the racing pilots assemble at Reno for a series of heats in different aircraft categories to see who is the fastest. With a few exceptions, the most exciting categories consist of World War 2 era aircraft. To be sure, these former warplanes in many cases have been substantially modified to eke out every last ounce of horsepower. While the basic airframes date from an earlier generation, the ongoing improvements usually result in slightly enhanced performance statistics for the piston-powered muscle machines in each succeeding year of the Reno races

Left Between the heats at Reno, it is airshow performers galore. Here the Eagles paint the sky. The Eagles are led by aerobatic great Charlie Hillard; wingmen are Gene Soucy and Paul Poberezny

Above Wheels retracting, Bruce Redding's AT-6 takes to the Reno sky

Overleaf Bunched at the pylon. Racing in the AT-6 class is often Reno's most exciting category because the airplanes are so evenly matched

Top left During a challenging contest, Charles Beck, in the striped tail SNJ-4, and Bruce Redding, in his red AT-6, appear to be flying formation

Left Bruce Redding's Texan and Nick Macy's *Six Cat* battle for position

Above Shoving it to the coals as the final pylon nears!

Top left Countless man-hours go into preparing and maintaining the racers at Reno. Here a crew tends to *Dash One*, an AT-6

Left This is Jim Good's colourful *Wildcatter*, an SNJ-5 based at Casper, Wyoming

Above *Tinker Toy* is the nickname for a Harvard Mk II. The nickname reflects the often creative artwork applied to Reno racing aircraft

Overleaf, main picture Hawker Sea Fury *Nuthin' Special* in an uncharacteristic quiet moment

Overleaf, inset The Sea Fury's mascot with flag of origin

65

Above Rick Brickert's well-known Unlimited class contender *Dreadnought* with the Nevada desert in the background

Top right A newcomer to Reno was *Maniyak*, a newly rebuilt Soviet Yak-11 from the Egyptian Air Force. Not considered a serious contender in the Unlimited class's gold heat, this Yak experienced mechanical difficulties that grounded it during the races. Nevertheless, its sleek lines and bright red paint job added a lot of colour and beauty to Reno's flight line

Right Ready to race! This silver Yak-11 belongs to Unlimited racer Robert Yancey and sports a very powerful Pratt

Top left Overpowered by the heavier iron, the dainty P-40 contributes a touch of charm and nostalgia to the races

Left The Unlimited champion—Bill 'Tiger' Destefani's greatly modified P-51 *Strega* ('witch' in Italian). Under a protective canopy, its crew goes to work. Everyone at Reno was amazed at how finely they tweaked *Strega's* Merlin engine

Above *The Healer*, one of the numerous P-51s at Reno, awaits the call for an Unlimited heat

Right Australian Guido Zuccoli's Fiat *Ciao Bella* takes a breather as spectators peer overhead from their perch atop one of the crew vans

72

Left *The Healer* edging out the Fiat G.59-B in one of the Unlimited heats

Overleaf, left Framed against the Reno landscape, the muscular looking P-51 *Stiletto* was a contender in the Unlimited class

Overleaf, right Ag pilot and World War 2 combat veteran Lefty Gardner, a fixture at Reno and on the airshow circuit, speeds by in his P-38 *White Lit'nin*. **Following pages** The sleek twin-boom design of the Lightning is evident as Lefty whisks past the famous Reno finishing pylon

Left Churning the air with near reckless abandon, these Sea Furies fight for extra inches!

Above Howard Pardue in the blue Bearcat and Skip Holm in the Sea Fury *Blind Man's Bluff* are seen here jockeying for position in a straightaway. Unfortunately, engine problems plagued *Blind Man's Bluff*

Overleaf Part of the Reno ritual is for each Unlimited racer's crew to tow their aircraft in front of the grandstands in a ceremony just prior to the last and most important heat—the Unlimited Gold. Here John Maloney gets the royal treatment as his crew tows his *Super Corsair*, a former Unlimited champ

Left Eliot Cross dives for speed in a highly modified Waco during an airshow interlude

Above The two wingwalking Wacos of Jimmy Franklin being pushed ever so delicately to the Reno flight line

Left The freakish looking Sikorsky Skycrane
demonstrates its water dispensing capabilities. A
refreshing sight on a hot day in the Nevada desert

Above Some of the old KC-97 military refuelling
tankers were converted to civilian fire bombers. Here
one makes a low level flyby

Overleaf, left Nose high in a simulated carrier
approach, this F-14 Tomcat passes slowly with gear
down and tailhook extended. Current military aircraft
fill some of the airshow slots at Reno

Overleaf, right Wings swept and afterburner ignited,
this Tomcat is the real speed champion at Reno

The legendary Robert A 'Bob' Hoover seems to pop up at just about every major airshow in the United States. While the typical airshow pilot may be satisfied to handle a lone warbird or high performance aircraft, Bob Hoover flies a stable of them. Having served as a test pilot for North American Aviation, he fittingly flies airplanes with roots in that company. From his T-28, crew members watch the airshow

Right 'Gentlemen, you have a race!' With these words uttered over the radio in his famous Mustang *Old Yeller*, Bob Hoover, by Reno tradition, starts the Unlimited heats. In this scene, he is performing a beautifully executed slow roll during a lapse in the racing

Below When the Reno spectators look up and see a Sabreliner business jet doing aerobatics they do not have to read the big green letters on the wings to know it must be Bob Hoover. The Sabreliner is shown during a slow roll

Rebel, rebel

The Confederate Air Force celebrated its Ghost Squadron's 13th anniversary in grand style with a 'Wings of Freedom' airshow at its home base in Harlingen, Texas. In addition to the spectacular collection of old warbirds, some contemporary military aircraft, as those seen here, fly in for the fun. The CAF calls Harlingen home and thereby it is the unofficial capital of the warbird movement. With unremitting fervour, the CAF maintains the world's largest flying collection of World War 2 aircraft. During the airshow season, examples from the collection appear on the circuit but at Harlingen they all come together for fantastic time!

91

Left When not flying his open cockpit biplane, Jimmy Franklin is zooming through the skies in his ominous looking Aerostar. Dubbed *Starship Pride*, the airplane is the centrepiece of an airshow act specially devised for children. One of Jimmy Franklin's partners on the flight line announces over the loudspeaker that the aircraft is piloted by Zar, a benevolent knight from the imaginary planet Zufrinia, who seeks support for his efforts to free his countrymen from dictatorial rule

Above Hold on! Loop coming up! In his more recognizable habitat, Jimmy Franklin is tearing up the sky with one of the world's leading wingwalkers, Johnny Kazian

No contest. An F-16 pointed directly at Harlingen's control tower

Left Everyone flying in an airshow is a celebrity. Young airshow enthusiasts obtain the autograph of a Texas based Army helicopter crewman

Overleaf, main picture The CAF's B-17 Flying Fortress *Texas Raiders* thunders overhead

Overleaf, inset A close-up of the Fort's nose art

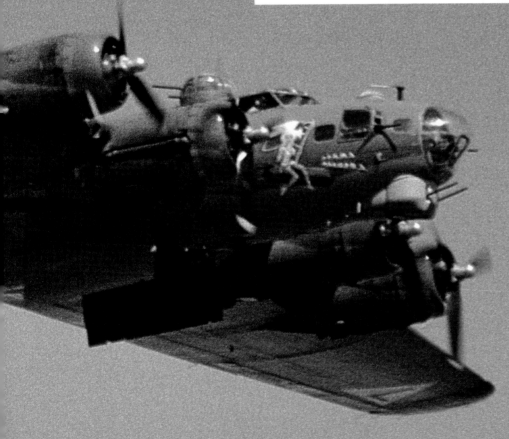

Above "*Fifi*" is the CAF's B-29

Top right The world's only flying Boeing B-29 Superfortress lumbers aloft

Right In tight formation are a few of the exotic warbirds in the CAF's amazing collection. To the left is the P-39 Airacobra in Soviet Air Force markings, reflecting the fact that nearly half of those built were provided to the Soviet Union under Lend Lease during World War 2. To the right is an A-20 Havoc, a low level bomber also known as the Boston by the RAF

The world's only flying Marauder, the CAF's B-26 takes a much needed drink of avgas from the ubiquitous CAF fuel truck

Left Reminiscent of the Pacific campaign, an Avenger rumbles past

Above An extremely rare SBD Dauntless stands out against the towering cumulus clouds on a blisteringly hot Gulf Coast day

Left *Tora! Tora! Tora!* Replica *Kate* torpedo bombers begin their dive as they approach airshow centre. One of the highlights at the annual CAF airshow is the dramatic re-creation of the Japanese attack on Pearl Harbor. As the make believe attackers rush by on their first bomb run, pyrotechnics experts on the ground detonate flame-producing explosives that throw swirling smoke into the air. Wave after wave of the mock invaders follow, swooping down and pulling up—quickly filling the blackened sky. It is controlled pandemonium, unlike any other airshow performance

Above One of the *Kate's* shows off its delightful camouflage—almost too pretty to cover an instrument of destruction

Above The swordfish looks about ready to go, but of course it remains latched

Right Replica *Zeros* circle their target—a predesignated spot in front of and safely distant from the airshow audience

Overleaf A classic strafing run! This better not be real!

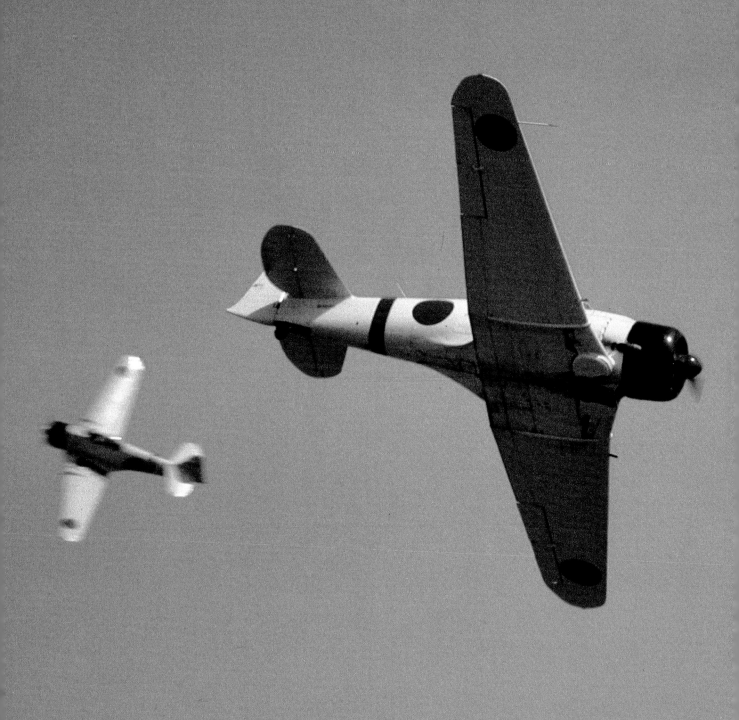

Team work

Left Helping to celebrate the 40th anniversary of Chuck Yeager's conquering of the speed of sound, the US Air Force's Thunderbirds produce a wondrously symmetrical shape against the crystal clear sky over Edwards Air Force Base. The military air demonstration teams signify something special during the airshow season. They are the no-nonsense performers who command the hottest machines in the sky. When they perform at a show, no one leaves until they have finished

Above The Thunderbirds' precision is evidence by this line abreast climb. It is almost as if some invisible puppeteer is pulling strings to keep all of the F-16s in proper position

113

During a tight diamond formation the Thunderbirds'
patriotic paint scheme on their upper fuselages and
tails can be seen

114

Above While rolled to knife edge flight, the 'thunderbird' motif painted on the underside is easily recognizable. The US Air Force chose this theme for its air demonstration team because according to American Indian lore the thunderbird possesses the ability to produce thunder, which of course is an ability sought by fighter pilots

Right The Thunderbirds make a delta pass, looking more like a single coordinated machine than six separate entities each with its own pilot in command

Above After their awesome display, the Thunderbirds taxi before an approving audience

Right Like their Air Force counterparts, the US Navy's Blue Angels travel across the country wowing airshow crowds. At the Willow Run Air Show in Michigan, the Blue Angels are seen in their tight diamond formation

Above Blue Angels on echelon parade in their new F/A-18 Hornets

Right Two dirty passes, side by side

Above This is the Blue Angels double farval. Two F/A-18s in the formation roll inverted so that half the formation flies positive while the remainder flies upside down

Right Stacked like pancakes! Only a few feet apart, the crack Naval aviators of the Blue Angels offer another definition of the word precision

Overleaf Not to be outdone by the American military air demonstration teams, the Canadian Forces display their excellent team, the Snowbirds, at over sixty airshows throughout North America. Seen here are all nine team members engaged in an aerial ballet at the Freedom Festival Air Show in Windsor, Ontario

Left The nine aircraft formation passes gracefully—
the symmetry of the lingering smoke trails restating
the extent of the team members' skill

Above A sure way to get an airshow crowd's
attention—allow two military team aircraft to fly at
each other with a high closure rate and to bank
away from each other at just the right moment. The
Snowbirds seem to enjoy producing multiple heart
palpitations among the spectators for they perform
this stunt numerous times during their routine. Their
mount, the indigenous CT-114 Tutor, is a reliable old
basic jet trainer

Overleaf The Snowbirds provide an elegant symbol
of comradeship in the sky

127